A+ books

Colors

Orange

Seeing Orange All around Us

by Sarah L. Schuette

Reading Consultant:
Elena Bodrova, Ph.D., Senior Consultant,
Mid-continent Research for Education and Learning

Capstone
press

Mankato, Minnesota

A+ Books are published by Capstone Press,
151 Good Counsel Drive, P.O. Box 669, Mankato, Minnesota 56002.
www.capstonepub.com

Printed in the United States of America in North Mankato, Minnesota.
032010
005743R

Library of Congress Cataloging-in-Publication Data
Schuette, Sarah L., 1976–
    Orange: seeing orange all around us / by Sarah L. Schuette.
    p. cm.—(Colors)
    Summary: Text and photographs describe common things that are orange, including carrots, pumpkins,
and basketballs.
    Includes bibliographical references and index.
    ISBN-13: 978-0-7368-1469-0 (hardcover)   ISBN-10: 0-7368-1469-8 (hardcover)
    ISBN-13: 978-0-7368-5066-7 (softcover pbk.)   ISBN-10: 0-7368-5066-X (softcover pbk.)
    1. Orange (Color)—Juvenile literature. [1. Orange (Color)] I. Title.
QC495.5 .S365 2003
535.6—dc21   2002000703

Created by the A+ Team
**Sarah L. Schuette, editor; Heather Kindseth, designer; Gary Sundermeyer, photographer;
Nancy White, photo stylist**

A+ Books thanks Michael Dahl for editorial assistance.

Note to Parents, Teachers, and Librarians
The Colors series uses full-color photographs and a nonfiction format to introduce children to the
world of color. *Orange* is designed to be read aloud to a pre-reader or to be read independently by
an early reader. Photographs and activities help early readers and listeners understand the text and
concepts discussed. The book encourages further learning by including the following sections:
Table of Contents, Words to Know, Read More, Internet Sites, and Index. Early readers may need
assistance using these features.

Table of Contents

Orange is bright.
Orange is round.

Carrots are vegetables
that grow under the
ground. We eat the root
of the carrot plant.

Orange grows under the ground.

Orange pumpkins grow on vines that twist along the ground. You can scoop out pumpkin seeds and carve faces in pumpkins.

Orange plumps
up in a patch.

Softball and baseball players catch balls in orange leather gloves. A good glove keeps players from hurting their hands.

Orange makes a winning catch.

12

Some leaves turn orange in the fall. The leaves dry up before falling off the tree.

Orange floats down from the trees.

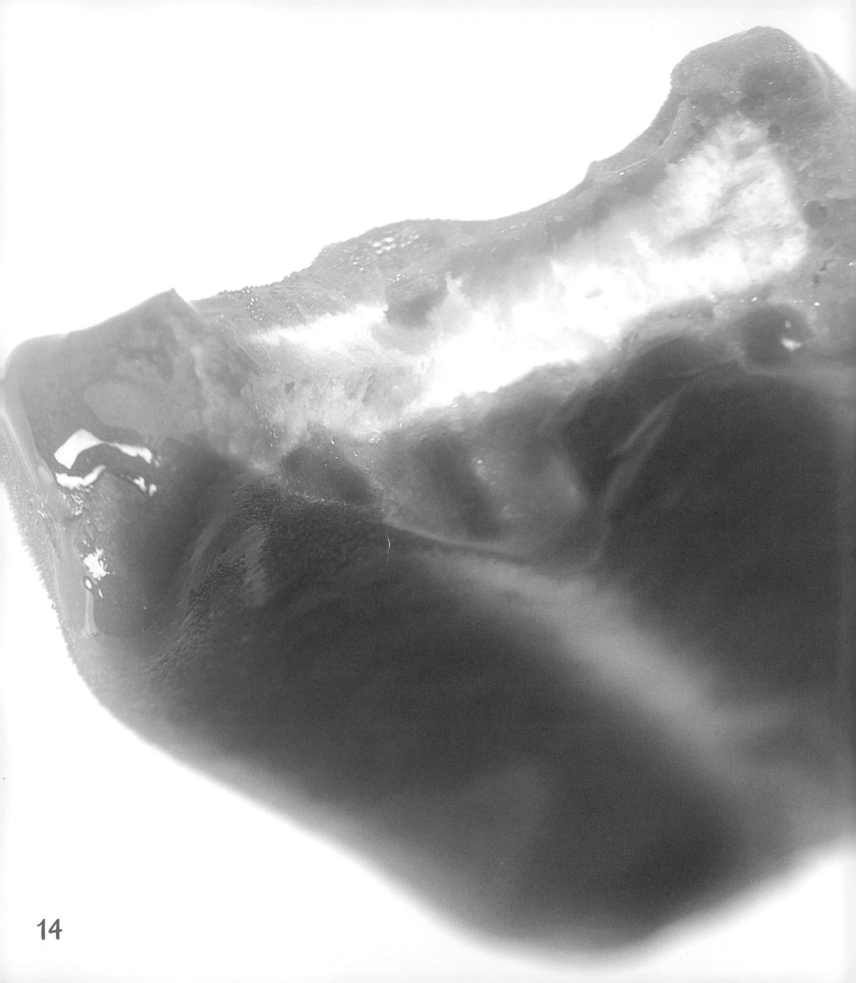

Frozen orange treats
taste good in warm
weather. They melt
in your mouth and
cool you down.

Orange can melt.
Orange can freeze.

Monarch butterflies are insects with four orange wings. These butterflies flap their wings slowly. They flutter through the air.

Orange flutters
above the grass.

Bright orange is an easy color to see. Orange cones help drivers pass by work areas safely.

Orange shows cars that they can pass.

Orange can spin.
Orange can bounce.

The first basketball
looked like a soccer
ball. Today, most
basketballs are orange.

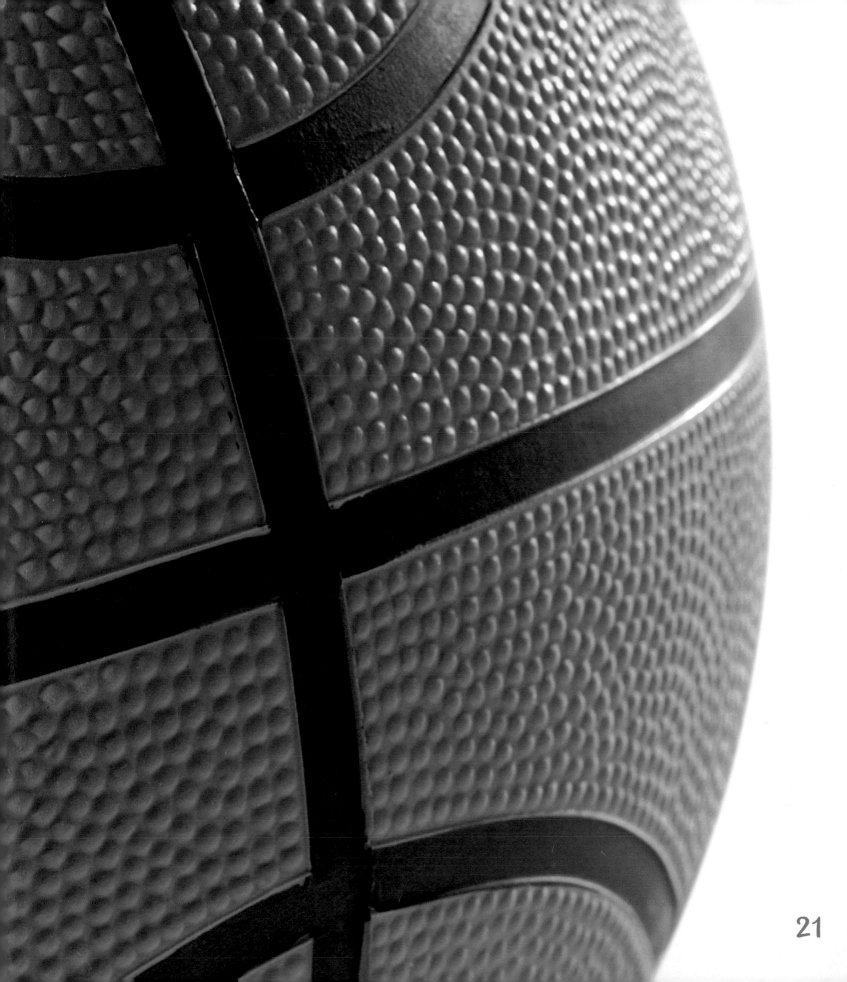

Tigers have orange
and black stripes.
Each tiger has its own
pattern of stripes.

Orange can prowl.
Orange can pounce.

Orange gives us crunchy snacks.

24

Crunchy orange snacks taste like cheddar cheese. Cheddar cheese is orange and is made from cow's milk.

Orange paddles.
Orange quacks!

Making Orange

Artists use a color wheel to know how to mix colors. Yellow, red, and blue are primary colors. They mix together to make secondary colors. Orange, purple, and green are the secondary colors they make. You can make orange by mixing yellow and red.

color wheel

You will need

2 spoonfuls of ketchup

1 large zipper-closure plastic bag

2 spoonfuls of mustard

1 Put the ketchup into the bag.

2 Next, put the mustard into the bag. Zip the bag closed.

3 Press your finger on top of the bag and mix the two colors together. See what shapes and designs you can make with orange in your bag.

Words to Know

butterfly—an insect with wings; butterflies can be many colors; there are more than 10,000 types of butterflies living in the world.

insect—a small animal with a hard outer shell, three body sections, and six legs; some insects have wings.

patch—a small area of ground used for growing things; people plant pumpkin seeds in a patch.

pattern—a repeating set of colors, shapes, or designs; no two tigers have the same pattern of stripes.

plump—to become fat or round in shape; ripe pumpkins are orange; they plump up when they are ready to be picked.

prowl—to move around quietly while looking for prey; tigers move very quietly in order to catch other animals to eat.

vine—a plant with a long stem that grows along the ground; vines can be leafy and green or woody and brown.

Read More

Pickering, Robin. *I Like Oranges.* Good Food. New York: Children's Press, 2000.

Salzmann, Mary Elizabeth. *Orange.* What Color Is It? Edina, Minn.: Abdo, 1999.

Winne, Joanne. *Orange in My World.* The World of Color. New York: Children's Press, 2000.

Internet Sites

FactHound offers a safe, fun way to find Internet sites related to this book. All of the sites on FactHound have been researched by our staff.

Here's how:
1. Visit *www.facthound.com*
2. Type in this special code 0736814698 for age-appropriate sites. Or enter a search word related to this book for a more general search.
3. Click on the **Fetch It** button.

FactHound will fetch the best sites for you!

Index